Weighing Light

Weighing Light

POEMS

Geoffrey Brock

WINNER OF THE NEW CRITERION POETRY PRIZE

Ivan R. Dee

CHICAGO 2005

*Funding for this year's New Criterion Poetry Prize
has been provided by the Drue Heinz Trust.*

www.ivanrdee.com

Library of Congress Cataloging-in-Publication Data:
Brock, Geoffrey, 1964–
  Weighing light : poems / Geoffrey Brock.
      p. cm.
  "Winner of the new Criterion Poetry Prize."
  ISBN 1-56663-667-1 (alk. paper)
  I. Title. PS3602.R623W45 2005

                              2005025354

Acknowledgments

I am grateful to the editors of the following publications, in which earlier versions of these poems (sometimes with different titles) first appeared: *32 Poems*: "Exercitia Spiritualia," "Father Countries"; *American Literary Review*: "Sinkholes"; *Blackbird: An Online Journal of Literature & the Arts* (blackbird.vcu.edu): "Abstraction"; *The Cortland Review*: "Genesis"; *Crab Orchard Review*: "The Starvers," "Transit Gloria Mundi"; *The Gettysburg Review*: "Her Voice When She Is Feeling Weak"; *Hellas: A Journal of Poetry and the Humanities*: "Vision (Sweet Recess)"; *The Hudson Review*: "The Familiar Itch," "For My Daughter," "My Austere and Lonely Office (Soliloquies)," "Odysseus Old," "The Upper Room"; *Literary Imagination*: "O Mother of Muses, O Father"; *The Literary Review*: "The Family Manse"; *Memorious: A Forum for New Verse and Poetics* (memorious.org): "The Male Mantis," "The Orpheus Variations"; *The Mississippi Review Online* (mississippireview.com): "Interview," "The Last Dinner Party," "Mon Chat, Mon Semblable," "Move"; *The New Criterion*: "Mezzo Cammin," "Ovid Old," "Weighing Light"; *New England Review*: "The Beautiful Animal," "The Last Suburbia," "The Man Outside," "The Royal Palms of South Florida," "Snake Bird at Rest"; *New Letters*: "The Cave Club," "Leaving Kansas"; *Paris Review*: "Telephone"; *Poetry*: "And Day Brought Back My Night," "Forever Street," "Snake Man"; *PN Review* (England): "Cold Pastoral," "Diretto," "Drive," "Eating

Carrots with Charlie Bernheimer," "Modern Romance," "No Despicable Gift," "The Photomancer," "Possum Hours," "Postscript," "You Are Here"; *Press*: "The Jolly Toper"; *Sewanee Theological Review*: "Northeaster"

The Philomathean Society Anthology In Honor of Daniel Hoffman: "Vision (Sweet Recess)"; *Verse Daily* (versedaily.com): "Father Countries"; *Writing Poems* (6th Ed.): "Move"; *The Year's Best Fantasy and Horror: Thirteenth Annual Collection*: "Odysseus Old"

Many thanks to the MacDowell Colony, the Millay Colony, and the Virginia Center for the Creative Arts for residencies during which some of these poems were written, and to the American Antiquarian Society, the Arizona Commission on the Arts, the Florida Arts Council, and the National Endowment for the Arts for fellowships supporting my poetry.

This book is for my parents, Van K. Brock and Frances Brock—poets themselves and my first poetry teachers. Among my later teachers, I am particularly indebted to Daniel Hoffman, Judy Moffett, William Logan, and Sidney Wade. I am also grateful to Sara Bullard, Lainie Decker, Kim Garcia, Holly Iglesias, Michael McShane, Randall Mann, Catherine Reid, Paul Shepherd, and Andrew Shields for close readings and inspiration over many years. I owe thanks to more people—including all my cohorts and teachers at the University of Florida's fine M.F.A. program and at Stanford's sublime Wallace Stegner program—than I can name.

And I owe more than I can name to Padma Viswanathan.

Contents

Weighing Light

Abstraction

It's coitus interruptus with the sweaty world.
It's the view from the window of the plane

As it gains altitude and the pines recede
Into forest—always it's the pull away.

The pull away from the darkness and the heat
Of a mother's bleeding body, toward cold light,

Toward names and language and desire and their
Majestic failures. It's love, it's death of love,

It's junk mail: see that blue truck shuddering
From my concrete curb, bearing this letter

For the Current Resident at your address?
And real death, too—the red-beaked gull we saw

Abstract a mullet from the surf and wheel
Across the iron-black sands of a nameless beach.

And Day Brought Back My Night

It was so simple: you came back to me
And I was happy. Nothing seemed to matter
But that. That you had gone away from me
And lived for days with him—it didn't matter.
That I had been left to care for our old dog
And house alone—couldn't have mattered less!
On all this, you and I and our happy dog
Agreed. We slept. The world was worriless.

I woke in the morning, brimming with old joys
Till the fact-checker showed up, late, for work
And started in: *Item: it's years, not days.*
Item: you had no dog. Item: she isn't back,
In fact, she just remarried. And oh yes, item: you
Left her, remember? I did? I did. (I do.)

The Beautiful Animal

By the time I recalled that it is also
terrifying, we had gone too far into
the charmed woods to return. It was then

the beautiful animal appeared in our path:
ribs jutting, moon-fed eyes moving
from me to you and back. If we show

none of the fear, it may tire of waiting
for the triggering flight, it may ask only
to lie between us and sleep, fur warm

on our skin, breath sweet on our necks
as it dreams of slaughter, as we dream
alternately of feeding and taming it

and of being the first to run. The woods
close tight around us, lying nested here
like spoons in a drawer of knives, to see

who wakes first, and from which dream.

Cold Pastoral

The single calf
in the wide field bleating

grieves for the high
weightless atmospheres

where he grazed on
darkness at the heart

of a herd of thousands—
on cloudplains of darkness,

endless and perfect
but for that sudden

brightness through which
he alone has fallen.

Drive

Headlights brush
Aside the night
As the painted
Flashes of white
By which I steer
Rush beneath me,
Always coming

And never here,
Always leaving
And never gone.
Night (old hound
I gave a bone
To once too often)
Circles around

To close in from
The rear—I press
Hard on the gas,
But nothing ahead
Grows any clearer
Than the dark glass
That is my mirror.

Diretto

Forgive my scrawl: I'm writing this in the near-dark
      So as not to wake you. I'm amazed you're sleeping;
I can't. Whenever we grind into some rural station,
      I wait for your eyes to tighten or to snap

Open with fright, with that *oh-shit-what's-happening* look
      That sometimes comes to them on sudden waking,
Even at home—if a cat, say, jumps from the bed,
      Tamping the floor, or the heater stutters on.

Your eyes stay shut but not still; they move beneath their lids
      To a rhythm as far beyond me as the landscapes
Of shadow that unreel themselves on the far side
      Of this drawn vinyl shade . . . We're slowing, again,

To a stop. Someone's shuffling off, dragging a bag—
      If you hear that, you hear it as something else,
And if you feel our gentle waking from inertia
      As the train moves again, you feel it elsewhere.

Someone's walking toward us—they try our door: it's locked.
      Selfish, I know, but I don't want to share
The sight of you asleep. In the next compartment a suitcase
      Chunks on the rack, then a sound like a struck match—

And I imagine cities blazing in your sleep.
　　I want to ask what country you're awake in,
What haunts you in that place, what ecstasies arouse you . . .
　　Everything wants to dream itself into something

Larger tonight: the train, this warm compartment, the seen
　　And unseen. Let's say they're just themselves. That you
Are here with me. And that these words are just a transcript
　　Of this, the night of your heroic sleep.

Eating Carrots with Charlie Bernheimer

We have stopped talking // about L'Histoire de la vérité . . .
—*Robert Hass*

The earth's breath rose from sidewalk grates
as I biked east, past campus, then across
the icy Schuykill, warmed only by the glow

of a finished dissertation, to meet Charlie
at a restaurant I could never have afforded.
Charlie, who came from money and spent it on art,

on elegant clothes that never quite matched
his boyish demeanor, and on glorious books:
at his parties they sighed at us as we opened them,

and we sighed back. (A year later, given weeks to live,
he called some students over to take their pick.)
This night he bought two meals at Le Bec Fin:

I don't recall the entrées (isn't that how it goes),
but one of the garnishes—ah, it's hard to say
how good it was: a flagrant orange dollop,

there as much for color as flavor. And Charlie
was overcome. *Taste this*, he pleaded: carrots, yes,
but transubstantiated as we could never have imagined.

After out-of-season raspberries, he called the chef
to praise—to *eulogize* the meal, then probed
the secrets of the dollop. —*It is nothing, monsieur:*

one steams the carrots until they are tender,
one bakes them until they are dried, one purées them
with a drop of honey . . .
                         —*But that can't be all!*

—*But yes, monsieur!*
                    —*No butter?*
                              —*Oh, perhaps*
(he winked) *a very small amount of butter, yes.*
There is so much, of course, that this story leaves out—

nearly everything. But six years later, when so much doesn't,
it's what returns: the famous chef still beaming,
and Charlie, gleeful, reaching toward his heart for a pen.

Epithalamium: Midsummer Convergence

for Michael and Seemee

The frisbee Michael throws rises and arcs
around the leafless plane tree. It is winter
and gray, it is a dozen years ago
and Philadelphia, and the white disc
is floating slowly toward me on a current
hidden from both of us. After it settles,
gentle as snow, into my hands, I'll answer,
perhaps retracing his arc, or describing
its complement around the phone pole, or
asserting something altogether new
and seeing what he makes of that.
                                        What's left
of afternoon will pass like this, until
our hands are blue, till all the air between us
has been sliced thin and every proposition
refuted or refined, till the light fails
and we retreat from the tree- and car-lined street
into the house on Osage Avenue
in which Michel-Bernard is roasting chicken —
and then, from there, to other houses elsewhere
in ever-diverging arcs.

But now, the disc
is floating toward me on its hidden current;
after it settles, gentle as snow, I'll answer
with motions that are charms or maybe mantras
(converge converge converge) against a world
bent on divergence—shouldn't arcs as small
as ours be shaped this simply? Soon the disc
that's floating toward me now on airy nothings
will vanish, and Michel-Bernard will vanish,
trailing the scent of chicken, and these plane trees,
these houses, all of Osage Avenue . . .

Yet there are those who won't have vanished yet,
others who will have bodied forth from ether,
and days to come that will end like comic plays:
in summertime, in Italy of course,
with everything converging in a rhyme.
On one such day, a dozen years from now,
we'll gather in a hall upon a hill,
Marino's mayor will play the Duke of Athens,
and Megan will play Snout, and as for me
I'll write some blank verse for the lovers' troth
and when we're drunk I'll read it to them both—
but we must wait for that.
                              For now, it's winter,
it's 48th and Osage, years ago,
Michel-Bernard is indoors roasting chicken,
and the white disc is arcing back toward Michael,
brimming on currents none of us can slow.
Soon, it will settle in his hands, like snow.

Exercitia Spiritualia

We met, like lovers in movies, on a quay
Beside the Seine. I was reading Foucault
And feeling smart. She called him *an assault*
On sense, and smiled. She was from Paraguay,

Was reading Saint Ignatius. Naiveté
Aroused her, so she guided me to Chartres
And Sacre Coeur, to obscure theatres
For passion plays—she was my exegete.

In Rome (for Paris hadn't been enough)
We took a room, made love on the worn parquet,
Then strolled to Sant'Ignazio. Strange duet:
Pilgrim and pagan, gazing, as though through

That ceiling's flatness, toward some epitome
Of hoped-for depth. I swore I saw a dome.

The Familiar Itch

If I happen to see a kid
Picking on his younger brother,
And if the little one looks cowed

Beyond what the moment warrants,
Then I figure the one knocks the shit
Out of the other when the parents

Are absent. Big brothers are such
Small gods. Seeing a scene like that,
I feel again the familiar itch

To get the kid alone somewhere,
Lean far into him with my eyes,
And slap him hard—and when the whir

In his ears dies, when fury, shame,
Shock, and fear all rise, to whisper
That is how he feels every time,

And leave him there, the way my father
(Youngest of two) left me, agape,
The last day I beat my brother.

The Family Manse

I.

These rooms breathe us. The shades of brief
    Versions of ourselves seethe
Around gray lines beneath the stairs
    That marked our heights. Each trace

Left somehow unerased will spark
    A flash—the faint claw-marks
On the door: Lady barks again.
    A tobacco-spit-stained

Corner of the porch: Ann, the maid,
    Arches her brows, explains
"Blacks spit black," and declines to share
    Her snuff. Knobbed scars in pairs

On the backyard oak's harrowed trunk:
    You and I climb pale rungs
To our fort, where the shrunken world
    Seemed for a while to yield.

II.

The fort's gone now, the world has grown,
        Lady and Ann are bones,
And this is ours. We own this lot.
        I've come to save what's not

Been thrown away or lost, before
        Pulling shut this warped door
For good. And on the floor, behind
        The chambers of a browned

Radiator, I find this black-
        And-white of us (on back:
"Xmas, '68"): Jackets tight,
        Tucked into that tie-dyed

Butterfly chair we liked so much,
        We watch snow from the porch.
We're curled together, touching like
        We love each other, while

Iowa, behind us, whitens. *That*
        Is what I'll save. And yet
Who knows what love means at that age?
        Perhaps it's just a stage

Boys go through, before rage sets in
        And we flare into men
And have these fallings-out with sleep.
        Still, it's what I must keep.

Father Countries

The first true human, Cain was born in sorrow.
Adam covered his ears as his son crowned;
Eve had fathomed her curse. Cain made no sound.
Cain the man cleared the chamomile and yarrow,
Conceived the scythe, the digging stick, the furrow,
Coaxed wheat and emmer from the wounded ground,
And sacrificed. Searching the sky, Cain found
Only God's vast back turned, spined by a sparrow.

The first to kill, the first to be unbrothered,
Cain ached to see God's face, even in anger.
Some sheep came wandering by; they ate the wheat.
A spotted moon rose; all the emmer withered.
Cain, soon to father countries of pure hunger,
Slaughtered a lamb and salted its bright meat.

For My Daughter

I hope that, once or twice, she's chosen last.
    I hope that some friend's trusted smile
Proves false, and that when she betrays a trust
    She hates herself a while.

I hope a handsome good-for-nothing boy
    Bruises her heart when her heart's strong.
I hope she isn't granted each wished-for joy,
    Occasionally is wrong,

And learns firsthand what loss is, and regret.
    I hope she faces prejudice.
I hope her world will still need saving—yet
    Not be as dire as this.

I hope her father's flaws are, in her eyes,
    Flaws. And if she has children too—
If anyone still does—I hope she dies
    Before the children do.

Forever Street

I met my withered mother
      Last night in a fever dream,
Her overcoat black as topsoil,
      Her hair a bluish gleam.

At first I didn't know her,
      The years had changed her so:
Her spine was bent like a comma,
      And every step was slow.

The concrete slabs of the sidewalk
      Lay broken and askew,
The roots of the ancient maples
      An unpaid wrecking crew,

And over the slabs lay a mantle
      Of fallen palmate leaves—
The bodiless hands of autumn
      With nothing up their sleeves.

I offered my arm to the woman,
      But she turned to me with scorn:
"What is it *now* that brings you
      To the street where you were born?

"The name of this street is Forever,
      And you haven't lived here for years;
The bulb in the streetlamp flickers,
      But everything's as it appears."

Her mouth clicked shut into silence
      Like a fisherman's pocketknife,
Her face became my daughter's,
      My daughter became my wife,

And they all sang "Happy Birthday"
      The way Marilyn sang it for Jack,
And their overcoat fell open,
      And I felt myself fall back.

Whoever she was now kissed me,
      Her lips like ice on my own;
I woke from the nightmare sweating—
      Burning, freezing, alone.

Genesis

One mango bent its branch
over the backyard pond.

    A water boatman sculled
        over a surface that held

        goldfish and faces,
        blue sky and the fruit,

and all I wanted was to touch it
    there on the side

    where the green skin
    had reddened in the sun.

In the beginning, it seemed
that simple.

Her Voice When She Is Feeling Weak

Her voice when she is feeling weak creates
A double pull in me, as a phone can
When it rings and rings and rings and no one else

Will answer it, and the machine that states
I'm not here right now is broken again,
And all day I've expected these two calls:

One from the creditor who likes to foretell
(With the shrill ardor of a true believer)
The grim details of my financial fate;

The other from a room in some hotel,
And all I want is to reach for the receiver
And hear her say she's fine and won't be late.

Interrogating Eros

He'd swoop up at the bus stop,
      in front of the girls,
and with a sharp finger to my sternum
      knock me back on my heels—

I never learned to expect it.
      He stole my lunches so often in those days
he grew fat. Soon
      there was no one his own size.

But then he'd act like my pal for a while
      and I'd always forgive him—
even later, even now that he's made me his partner
      in crime. I think I must love him.

But what a chicken-hearted boy he can be!
      See for yourselves:
here we are now, a jittery pair
      of petty thieves

sweating in our twin interrogation rooms.
      And there (think Dennis Franz)
looms the bad cop, at whose first word,
      at whose first serrated glance

my friend's crest will fall and he'll pin some tale
        on me. And here I sit, reciting
the script he wrote—"it was broken
        already when we arrived,

we didn't think it would be missed," and so forth—
        which by now I know by heart.
But my cops, a couple of Barney Fifes,
        just chuckle and fart

and wink at the two-way mirror.
        (*Is she observing this?*
I suddenly think to ask. *Are you out there?*
        I say to my image in the glass.)

Later, he'll shove his sharp fingers deep in his pockets
        as we pass in the hall.
He'll toddle freely and wholly out of this precinct.
        There won't be any trace of her at all.

Jolly Toper

That twinkle in his eyes is glassiness: he's dazed.
His left hand holds a cup of wine; his right is raised
As if to greet a friend who might
Buy drinks—a friend, however, whose name he hasn't quite
Remembered yet. (I fear he never will.)
Or else he simply tires of standing there so long, so still,
In that silly wide-brimmed hat, waiting
For Hals to finish painting.

These slashing brush strokes seem a moment's labor now.
But sweat gleams on the toper's brow,
And his mouth, half-open in what must have begun as a smile,
Has been dry a great while.
How long, he seems to be thinking,
Till I may lift this heavy glass and finish drinking?

The Last Dinner Party

for Kim Garcia

The usual sounds: forks on plates, and voices,
and the easy laughter of friends together—and I,
too, am laughing, and happy, and a little drunk . . .

Then I am walking down a hall and closing a door,
muting the laughter, then leaning toward a mirror
in which I see myself three times: the bloated visage

that rises from my neck, and the eyeless twin
that floats in the jar of each pupil. When I return
to the table of my friends, the silence comes along

and sits with me until Kim says something funny
and I can't help laughing again, and then David
says something even funnier, and then Frank too,

and we're on some kind of roll, gathering threads
from earlier conversations and weaving them in,
weaving the whole evening into one tight fabric

that we wrap around ourselves like a shared belief,
and for a few graceful moments we are gaining on time,
all of us laughing and blinking tears from our eyes.

The Last Suburbia

You've come to lie here by this stand of ash.
The hard clay path behind you is a long
Abrasion arcing away, over the swell

And down toward unseen rows of houses where
Neighbors settle for dinner and their children
Chatter and their dogs dig toward open fields.

Cemeteries, you said, were the first suburbias.
Above you, a jay cavils in the branches.
Arterial light burns the burnished leaves.

Where can we turn from here? Even the jay
Falls silent. I've come because, in a time zone
Far from this one, your lover's dying is over.

If I believed what you, at the end, believed,
I'd say he's on his way to see you—but
I can't believe. I don't know why I've come.

Cicadas hum their scratched-brass elegies
As dry, unhinging winds shake the tall trees.
And all around me, winged seeds descend.

The Male Mantis

Let me explain in terms you'll understand:
Picture a boy who, starved for love, has planned
And executed another household crime,
And now his mother has discovered him

And glowers down from the bright ceiling where
Her face is the dark sun, and the ear-whir
Of fear and desire mounts, for soon she'll speak
His name with passion and meet his pale dry cheek

With the full sail of her hand, loosing the tears
Of shame and gratitude—all the boy cares
To know of bliss. And then forget his trauma
With its dysfunctional-family melodrama,

And think of me with her to whom all heads
Bow as to the body's harshest, best-loved gods.

The Man Outside

Her house, illuminating the moonlessness,
Glows, even now, through each of its openings.
            Light soaks the undersides of cedars.
        Silhouettes shift in their frames. Around them,

Frogs chant desire's precarious choruses;
Field crickets carve their wings into night music;
            Wind bends the branches of gardenias,
        Bearing the scent of their dying to me.

One silhouette remains. It extinguishes
One room, then two, till darkness is general.
            Wind bears the sadness of gardenias.
        Later, from deep in the woods, an owl calls;

White birds desert my heart's dark tree, silently.
Frogs chant and crickets carve. It is only in
            Such dark that fainter stars seem brilliant.
        Lying on dampening grass, I find them.

Mezzo Cammin

Today, as I jogged down the center line
Of a closed-off, rain-glossed road, lost in a rhythm,
The memory of a boy returned: fifteen

Or so, barefoot in faded cut-off jeans,
Sprinting past neighbors' houses, tears drifting
Into his ears, heart yanking at its seams—

He hoped they'd rip and didn't slow at all
For more than a mile. After crossing Mission,
The boy collapsed beneath an oak, his whole

Body one cramp. (But later the secret smile,
Imagining Guinness there—the clock-men stunned!)
Twenty years gone, that race so vivid still,

Yet I can't for the life of me recall the gun:
Who was it, or what, that made me start to run?

Modern Romance

Back at her place after an evening
Conjured by a modern in chivalric style,
She twisted her hair into a rope
And held it as she told him, with a smile

A skilled mortician might have fashioned,
The scientific name for what she had.
Soon (not the evening of her telling
But soon) they were lying in her bed,

Her hair now a dark corona around her head,
And only the thinnest armor between them—
He would have taken that off, too,
For her, but she said *no no no*, for him.

Mon Chat, Mon Semblable

We met, we fell in bed, we got two cats.
All fall we fucked with noisy desperation.
Our colors changed. We shed our leaves. We snowed
And salted all the roads. Then the birds left,

And what's-his-name came back and now you're gone,
Leaving only the cat you named for me
(Which pines now for the one you named for you)
To prove this winter different from the last.

More Light Verse

Controlled Burn

The benefits are clear: its scope is limited;
      Most important things, though scorched,
      Are left standing; soil is enriched.
The trick, I find, is holding the perimeter.

Salt and Battery

These erstwhile better halves corrode and leak.
He drips his pity-me on my dry sleeves.
She tries to fuck his friends — it's how she grieves.
Lawyers circle. Their two-year-old won't speak.

The Day Before Their Suicide

The patient Eva, pink with shame and pride,
      Became, at last, his blushing bride.
For their brief honeymoon, they lied and lied
      As Eva laughed and Adolf cried.

Move

Try driving twenty hours in a truck,
Your life a sprawl of boxes chasing you,
Only a few of them light. Add bad luck:

The radio doesn't work; the cat with whom
You share the cab decides, in hour one,
To piss in her cage (she is, we can assume,

As scared as you are); and—since these streaks run
In threes—it starts to rain. Now, with a mere
Thousand miles to go, with a vague sun

Rising and glaring through the buggy smear,
Say goodbye to those days, and praise the truck,
And praise the cat, and grip the wheel and steer.

Mundane Comedies

I. The Cave Club

The truckers, college boys, and paraplegics
Suck on their cokes and smoke like prisoners
By the small stage, where naked women dance.

A life-size blue and orange hummingbird
Flits inches from my face on the tanned ass
Of a blonde dancer, who (as if it were

A real mosquito) slaps it, turns around,
And laughs, "S'okay to smile, ya know." I smile.
The paraplegic next to me drags hard

On a filterless that's clipped to a dead hand.
His good hand thrusts a bill at me: "You mind?"
Hummingbird pauses, poised above the blooms

Of cash that ring the thigh below its reach.
Pulling her garter back, I slide in two bills
As the song ends. She slumps a little, turns

And asks, "You know about our private dances?"
As if I haven't seen the row of rooms
Walled with translucent plexiglass, or stared,

36

Enthralled, at their refracting shadows. "No,"
I say, "I don't," so she begins explaining
As a nice waitress would the soup du jour.

Just then the paraplegic's beeper chirps.
"Wife's here," he whispers, as he puts his chair
Into reverse. I follow in his wake,

And in the dark lot watch as a glowing van
Extends its metal arms to take him in.

II. Leaving Kansas

Having just driven thirteen hundred miles
To see my soon-to-be-ex-wife again,
Having retraced the broad arc of our years

In weekend miniature (romantic meals,
A Chekhov play that ended with a gun,
A talk in the park, late wine, sober tears),

And having now regained the solitude
Of roads, I find once more the universe
Personalized for me: the weather: clouds

Like thick gauze over the heartland, then rain;
The radio: Greg Brown's "Just By Myself,"
Ferron's "Ain't Life a Brook" (which makes me think

Of a rhyme I wrote once, when it wasn't true:
"Nothing else can now go wrong, / unless,
Of course, they play our song"); the roadsigns, too:

Some clever, like the creek named *Perche* near
Columbia, and some not, like Paducah's
Husband Road. How can strangers wear

This world that fits me like a tailored hairshirt?
How, for example, can the passengers
In that speeding Odyssey ever hope to get

The shitty inside jokes around us? the *pathos*?
If I were less worn out by the world's wit,
I might feel special. But I'm not half home

And it's full dark, and vacillating overhead
The weak stars, most of which, I've heard, are dead.

III. Interview

"Well now if that don't just beat all," God says,
Gazing across the field at a knot of men
Arguing outside the tent. He seems

Tired; evening has fallen and many remain
To be interviewed. "Uh, yessir, it sure does,"
I stammer, handing him my application

And standing by the folding metal chair
That faces his. "So, Mr. — " But a cry
Cuts him off, and he rises to his feet,

Flustered. One man lies prostrate on the ground;
The rest have darted back inside the tent.
A gust of wind disturbs God's hair, his robe.

I cringe, expecting—what? Minutes pass.
"Your application," he resumes, "I thought—
I'm sure I set it here when I stood up."

There's nothing here but us, two empty chairs,
And sun-baked earth. He checks his pockets—nothing.
He turns, chagrined but not apologetic,

Smiles, and tells me: "You'll have to come on back
Some other time." I thank him and set out,
Sad but relieved, toward the swaying trees,

Now black against the darkening plain of sky.
"Good luck," he calls to me. As I glance back,
I see a woman emerge from the tent, sidestep

The body, and begin her trudge toward God,
Pale application flapping in her hands.

My Austere and Lonely Office (Soliloquies)

The Ashtray

Back then, I hated my job:
the heat, the mess, the smell.
Now my life's too clean, too tame:
I am the Keeper of Paperclips,
and I burn for the days of flame.

The Clock

I have three misshapen hands: the first hand
is the second hand, the second hand
is the minute hand, and the third hand
(the minute one) is the hour hand.
I can never keep them straight.

The Cordless Phone (Ringing)

I know, for what it's worth,
the sacred secrets of lovers
and felons, of prostitutes
and poets, but can repeat
only this ragged cry I've known since birth.

The Incense Burner

I think
the ashtray
has a crush on me—
I'll send up
a signal.

The Letter Opener

I long to be a tempered sword, or even a knife
with a real edge. With every envelope
I open, I imagine bright flesh
rending, my thin body
bathed in blood.

The Mechanical Pencil

Gray matter funnels
through me and out,
translates itself into
strange abstractions.
This peristalsis is all.

The Paperclips (In Unison)

If you find the Stapler's governing philosophy
unsettling, even fascistic (as *we* do), then consider
that our gentler methodology allows you to form
more peaceful unions, looser confederations,
and protects each member from harm.

The Scissors

I am plural. To become one
with my purpose, I must cut
something in two. This is how

I am made. Divided against my
self, I want everything divided.

The Stapler

The many who have become one in my embrace
can never deny their common bond, it's true,
or forget
their place,
but I see order, not violence, in that—don't you?

The Wineglass

Only when I am full of wine
do I recall how empty I have been.
And only when I recall how empty I've been
do I know how empty I'll be again.
Only when I am full of wine.

No Despicable Gift

The solstice in December, watershed
Of winter, beyond which light will drain toward summer
And days collect like snow on mountain roads:

First white, then muddy, rinsing down at last
With the first rains toward dull fields and thin rivers,
Until, each year, we find ourselves forgetting

We're older, going down again to the swollen river,
In the golden air, among the children, to offer
Our slow feet the quickening gift of water.

Northeaster

New snow fell hard on old all yesterday,
clumping thick on thin branches,
                                    bending them
and often whole trees down as if to pray
for sun.
          In the cathedral of that storm,

the only sounds above the snow that breathed
in godlike endless exhalation came
from the weak pines —
                          their rendings lightning sheathed,
their muffled landings distant thunder's rhyme.

Today no sun,
              but warmer, drier weather,
and the strong spent all morning letting go:
first one branch startled up,
                              and then another,

forgetting grief,
                  dropping their loads of snow,
each tree a dance,
                    the woods a thumping riot —
and now they stand green-gowned again,
                                      and quiet.

O Mother of Muses, O Father

"What mnemonic will you use?"
      I chirped, as if a connoisseur
of memory aids, as if the chance
      to choose between a Post-It Note
on the spattered bathroom mirror
      and a watch alarm he doesn't hear
were a win-win, like the Chez Pierre
      dessert menu (which he's no longer
allowed even to hold) used to be,
      before the diabetes and these pills
I want him to remember to take.
      But he's not too old to see through
false cheer:
          "What mnemonic indeed,"
he intoned. "And what mnemonic
will remind me to shave each morning,
      to salve these dried-out hands and comb
this wayward hair. O Mnemosyne,"
      he actually said, "what mnemonic
will remind me to breathe in my sleep,
      and to wake from sleep, and to write
a poem before I go again to bed?"

Odysseus Old

a sequel to MacLeish's "Calypso's Island"

In darker hours, I try recalling why
I left her. Gazing at a distant mast
or at a girl, I'll call back that lost island

of permanent sun, that woman immune to the passage
of all that passes. Memory's a ragged sail,
and years have faded to a wash of gasping

fascination: long months mapping the pale
shores of her skin, the smooth peninsulas,
the inlets; then the roads into her frailer

interior. Calypso frail? She was.
When told she had to let me go, such tears!
But loss couldn't mean for her what it does

for us, I reasoned. This, like much else, sheer
vanity. I was bored, and blessed or cursed
to know Penelope still waited here.

That faithfulness, ambrosia-sweet at first,
maddened me later on. Wasn't she human?
Didn't lack of water make her thirsty?

And am I so weak, who float through this dry room
nightly, dreaming water? If offered again—
but just what was I offered? And by whom?

No matter. This one offers all a mortal can
and more, and still this glooming. For how should I,
who once was envied by every Ithacan,

whose naked ears have known the song of sirens,
and who now am neither sung to by beauty nor envied,
be glad? I chose this, chose to slowly die.

And chose the woman sleeping by that window,
her gray hair silvering in the moon's weak light.
Her eyes flicker beneath their lids. Her fingers

twitch and clutch, as with some inward sight
she weaves and unweaves me, her days, this night.

Orpheus Variations

1. In Which He Turns With Intent

When we were almost out,
All I could think
Was *they can't really let me take her—*

Can they? And when I heard
The rasp of her shade on
A fern near the cave mouth,

I knew she was still there,
I had to turn,
I knew I couldn't bring her back,

Because it wasn't her
But grief that I loved with
Such passion that kingdoms

Were moved by its sad music.
Should the source
Prove hollow, then the music must.

And if I now shun women,
It's not for Eurydice's
Sake, but for theirs.

2. In Which He Turns Inward

Somewhere in the night a woman
Carried a burden into the lake
As snow settled like sleep. Cars turning

Onto the shore road threw out ropes
Of fraying light. And I remember
The radio in her apartment

Clearing its throat for days, her phone
Ringing, the sun gleaming ornately
On the cold white skin of the city.

When family came for her things,
Their narrow voices widened and widened
Like the pupils of trapped animals.

Of all the tricks of memory, the cruelest
Is accuracy. In the empty street
Below me, a limo passes, bass

Pulsing, the rest of its song lost.
As clouds of exhaust rise toward rows
Of halogen moons, I hear the door

That's always gently clicking shut
Behind me, find myself climbing,
Once more, my incomplete conception

Of her skirt-covered thighs, uncovering
All the lies I should have told her.

3. In Which He Never Turns

Emerging, my flesh firming again, I gasped
      Like a fish in the scalding air. I touched my face
      And blinked until the wall of light gave way
To shapes: a tree, and beside the tree a man,

Kneeling and weeping. Then the words returned:
      Weeping and *man* and *tree*. And like a tide
      Flowing back to a marsh across cracked mud,
My thick blood moved again. My ankle hurt.

His music, for a time, was a light thing
      Balancing the exhausting gravity of flesh.
But sadness always was his heart's true song,
      And one day, after a flimsy argument,

His flat *I wish I'd never come for you*
Brushed past my own *I wish you'd never too.*

4. In Which He Turns, Afterward, to a Young Man

The past—that's where you'll find your paradise.
      Why look here? Or think now about the cost?

I found my own in what I thought was hell,
      But only after I, alone, had crossed

Back. Whatever lies before you now
      Won't have been paradise until it's lost.

5. In Which He Turns Outward

He heard her brush against a fern,
And though he didn't mean to turn,
He turned; she vanished into mist.

Clutching at air, he woke and found her,
Breathing, beside him in their bed.
He felt as though he'd risen from

Deep water, heart thrashing the tight
Drum of his lungs, into this air
That tasted of salt and absolution.

He slipped soundlessly from their bed,
Walked down the hall, past the glossy
(Framed like some ancestral portrait)

Of him on stage with his old band,
Into the kitchen, where he brewed
A pot of coffee, took two cups

From the cabinet, and brought them back
To the dark room, their tails of vapor
Rising and curling quickly away.

Ovid Old

I.

        As a pale gauze
rose over Asia, he awoke
        surrounded by, not Rome,
        but huts, hanging
like tattered effigies of home
        from threads of cedar smoke;

        Europe was dark.
The woman by him also woke,
        gently helped him to stand,
        wrapped him in fur,
and led him outside by the hand
        to see the sun's great yolk

        push up against
the horizon's rim. After it broke
        and bled into the bowl
        of the Black Sea,
it rose again, transformed and whole.
        For minutes, neither spoke.

II.

"Time," he recited,
"tames the bullock to the yoke."
He laughed, more blithe than bitter,
the way he did
these days when he could find no fitter
punchline to some old joke

than himself. The woman
knew the laugh if not the joke,
the moods if not the meanings
of his strange words,
uttered aloud, to no one—keenings
that once had made him choke

with grief, but that
evolved, as Daphne's cries (a cloak
of bark abrading her body)
gave way to birdsong
in her branches. Some things no god
or Caesar can revoke.

The Photomancer

The signs, my dear, are there:
Notice how he is standing
In shade and you in sunlight,

And see that snow-capped peak
That hovers over you
Like a dunce hat? When it melts,

As it must, who'll be dry
And who drenched? Your white dress
Is all grace; but that tux—

A lotus blooming beside
Some scrub. And mark the shadow
Cast on his cheek by his nose:

An arrow heading straight
For your temple (and not, I think,
To worship). You, meanwhile,

Are leaning toward this blur
At the frame's edge—
                    how should
I know? A cloud of gnats?

The photographer's errant finger?
No, dear, that's no person;
Two figures only are present:

Your groom, smaller than life,
And you, brilliant and tall.
No, no, no, I assure you:

I am not here at all.

Possum Hour

Worn down by relentless
      small talk, and despite
his terrible breath
      and unbearable self-regard,
I gave in—it was easier
      than fighting him off:
I let morning take me

right here on the couch,
      where he's had his way
with me all afternoon,
      position after sordid
position, not tiring
      even now as evening
presses his possum

face to the glass
      awaiting his turn,
and the TV continues
      to watch me, transfixed,
and studio audiences,
      one after another,
jeer and applaud.

Postscript

They say Odysseus in later life
Would get Penelope to tie him down
And sing, as if she weren't his aging wife,

The sort of songs in which a man can drown.
To her, his longing was a gutting-knife,
And when she lifted up her woven gown,

It wasn't for him at all, and when she shuddered,
She was remembering the suitors he had slaughtered.

The Rat Snake Gospel

Her torpor (age?
Or a cold conspiracy
Of blood and springwater?) and size (heroic
In these times
Of progress) make her an ungainly

Éminence grise,
As do the milky blue domes
Of her eyes. From her chin hangs a second chin,
A lucent
Gray beard; from her nose rises a comb

Of peeling scales.
Gripping her throat with one hand,
I coax dead skin back, unmasking a new stare,
Bright and dark,
That fixes me as if to contend:

I'm not Evil's
Local host, nor a gray hair
Plucked from Medusa's scalp, nor a spotted Jove
Come to rape
Deo's daughter; I'm not Freud's nightmare,

Nor even this
Anti-myth—leave me alone!
As I clasp her old skin like a stocking's hem,
She squirms free
To scallop her way toward the bright stones.

The Royal Palms of South Florida

They line the streets like stoic palace guards
Stripped of all their pomp, or a colonnade
Of big-haired caryatids with nothing but porches

Of sky to support. Entasis gentles each trunk
Like a slight paunch, and fronds float in the air
As a catch of catfish, strung to a dock

And forgotten, might float, ghostly and skeletal,
After a few days in the Intracoastal.
They look like local South Americas

To renegade parakeets, and their gray trunks
Are endless lizard skyways, paved with dirty,
Lichened cement. They could be flagstaffs flying

Wind-shredded flags, or extras in a movie
About exiled rulers in a dull new world.

Sinkholes

News that the earth has opened again
     And swallowed someone's Buick
Pleases us, proves there is no terra
     Firma, not in karst country;
The day gains a sexy patina
     Of danger. That's why Chicken
Little tells those tales about the sky,

     Why we love storms and Hitchcock:
We *want* to know a tame sidewalk could
     Morph and swallow us alive.
Sinkholes, at least when the ulcer's fresh
     (When the astonished traffic
Balks, or when boles lie like the pillars
     Of a sacked temple), forestall

All the seize-the-day saws, and even
     Healed—calm and green as a pond
And full of bathers—they can arouse
     Small frissons: look at them as
Great cupolas inverted, thick shafts
     Of implacable darkness
Rising from each buried oculus.

Snake Bird at Rest

Neck a slack snare, each naked feather soaked,
He clutches a low oak branch, wings stretched wide,
Gorged to the gullet with gravid sunfish and fry
Flashing around him in the tannin-cloaked

Waters of recall, which are darkening now
As water darkens after the beak's thin
Gold awl punches its hole in the lake's skin
And body plunges through body, fluent, down,

Till nothing's left for him but this light wind
Blowing a lone cloud toward the bank, a brace
Of oily mallards, rumps thrust up, and weight—
Such tiresome weight! Feeling his thin bones bend,

He tilts a green-ringed eye toward the spark of a tail
As sun retouches each of the lake's glittering scales.

Snake Man

I in your presence resemble a hognose snake
        Lying on the spadelike scales

Of its back, in farinaceous dust, like a rope
        Of dough. And when you flip me

With the toe of a shoe, I do not (oh no) flip
        Back, for unlike that saphead

The hognose, I know many positions in which
        To be dead. And when you smile

To describe, in your up-to-date patois, all love
        As aleatory, or

Desire and indifference as twin winnowers,
        Then I with my upturned nose

(Keeping my venom even then to myself) hiss
        Softly at your shoelaces.

Speak Now (Soliloquies)

The Bouquet

No one ever talks about
what becomes of the bride's bouquet
after I've been flung and caught
by blossoming girls on a sunny day.
(They know, of course. They just can't bear to say.)

The Cake Statuette

We've posed all day in formal dress,
feet iced, arms intertwined.
And though you'd never guess
from our perfect, plastic smiles,
we mind.

A Champagne Flute (Slightly Drunk)

You don't have to be Phi Beta Kappa
to look at this pair and know
true love is sometimes *faux*.
(It ain't champagne, *mon frère*,
if the grapes were grown in Napa.)

The Garter

The pulse and musk of her in this dark tent—
life will never again be as good as this.
After he hikes the dress, what then? A year or
maybe two (brief afterglow of bliss!)
of hanging limply from his rear-view mirror.

The Getaway Car

I've never looked so dumb in all my life.
I thought the man had balls.
I thought he *liked* things my way.
A wife! Before we reach Niagara Falls
I swear I'll drop my trannie on the highway.

The Knife

Let's admit impediments:
I tire of my diet of cake and more cake.
What about some cheese, some steak?
(Once I nicked a bride's tongue, just to try it—
I haven't been sharpened since.)

The Photographer's Camera

These gigs are just to pay the bills, you know?
I'm actually an artist. Experimental?
I did once have a show, which went quite well.
The thing is, though, I'm into the accidental—
my stuff's not *decorative* enough to sell.

The Rice (in Dirge-Like Unison)

We have been known to feed
the poor. Yet here we're thrown
into the laughing, shouting faces of the rich…
And if we sprout, it's only as a weed
rising from birdshit in a ditch.

The Veil

I'm gifted: I see them as they are,
yet hide them from their spouse-to-be.
Until I'm lifted, what they mostly see
(as each embroiders the other's face
with swatches of my lace) is me.

The Wedding Ring

I'm glad you like my rocks.
But I feel what Snow White
must have felt when her prince
finally showed: delighted
just to get out of that damn box.

The Starvers

Two bull elk lay dead in the snow, antlers
locked. It was October, rutting season,

the Canadian hills were splotched like the sky
with white, and you stood there beside me,

repulsed by the carcasses, by the way
their elk eyes stared dully toward the earth,

the glaze of their astonishment fading.
Just like men, you said, turning

to walk back to the truck, putting that distance
between us. I stayed a while, and winters came,

and summers. I don't think of you often.
But when the weather's right, I can see the bulls

sinking down together, wet nostrils flaring,
to starve. The does wandering away.

The sky like this one, lurid blue and tilted sharply,
and that single shapely cloud spilling off.

Stick

Sunlit and motionless, the copperhead
        Lies on the sandy bed
Of a stream that, but for a glass veneer,

Is nearly dry. My dog's too close; I call her
        And throw a fetching stick
Back up the gully, far from the scent of snake.

        How easily this earth gives
Beneath my boots as I slope down the bank—
I should, perhaps, but do not, think of flesh.

        I'm drawn as if by a leash
(I always have been drawn to them like this)
Over the sand that shows where each paw sank

To where she milled and turned, and then beyond,
        Field-guide image in mind:
Dark, fractured hourglass on a pale ground.

I'll catch it, cage it, fatten it on mice—
        Then tire of playing god
And set it free. I'm thinking how to pin it,

When I at last perceive, around my feet,
     The scattered bones and tusks,
Of a wild boar. And this is when the world

Quietly changed: pines leaned and their roots curled,
     Tilting the forest floor—
I nearly lost my balance looking down

     At the snake lying before me:
No copperhead at all: merely the play
Of shadows over polished vertebrae.

In the shifted light, adrenalin draining out,
     My own bones felt rinsed clean.
My wagging dog was back, dirty and wet

From combing the sticky woods for the one stick.
     She set it by a bone,
As if to make a field guide of her own.

Telephone

Only in Europe is it enjoyed by telephone.
—Les Murray, "Shower"

Loaf of bread or sheep's
    head, rubber-nubbed
for traction on flatnesses
    or frogged to a kitchen wall;
poker-faced bearer of job offers
    and death notices; deaf,
stuttering house-servant
    in whose presence everyone
speaks freely; married couple,
    vows forever tangling, or
cool detached lover who by day
    roams from room to room
spouseless and priapic,
    only to return at night,
exhausted; mask for the ugly
    and veil for the naked;
ear-to-shoulder fastener;
    cat pillow; teenager goiter;
shortest distance between
    two points; and Europeans
use it in the shower.

Tennessee in Florida (Old Fussy)

At the 1979 world premier of Tennessee Williams's Tiger Tail

He asked his agent, in a drawl as thick
As Blanche DuBois's, *Just where the hell'd'you book me?*
He screeched commands: *Aunt Rose must be recast!*
And *Someone drive me to a fine men's store—*
If Gainesville has one—*I need shoes.* He skipped
The mayor's dinner in his honor, quipping
What good are keys to unlocked towns? when found
Drunk with a waiter in the Hilton bar.
(Desire, as Blanche declared, or death.) That night
The preview flopped: he squawked at all the jokes
Early. Backstage, he gushed *Aunt Rose was brilliant!*
Then asked to hold the bird: *Old Fussy's based*
On a real hen, a pet I doted on—
Until the day the preacher came to dinner.

Transit Gloria Mundi

Philadelphia

It will be dark when I descend
From my apartment, and dark still
When I sidestep the daily blend

Of bliss debris and the body steaming on its grill,
And dark when I descend below the wind
To enter the warm animal that will bear

Me to 40th Street, where it will shrill
Out of the dark mouth of its lair
Into the early morning's enlightening air.

Houston

Here in the black macadam sluiceways
Of five o'clock, a mottled shoal
Of glass-and-metals hovers in a daze

Of idling heat, each painted shell
Sweating light. Mute swan-necked streetlamps raise
Their lowered heads above their captive

Audience, and from behind a swell
Of offices, a traffic helicopter
Shudders toward us like some beakless raptor.

Las Vegas

Hiking up, we saw nothing of the plains
But the pale yellow underbelly
Of the heaped cumulus above them, which rained

A light so pure and pale it seemed angelic.
But when we reached the mesa, a simmering lake
Of neon shocked the dark and shorted all

The stars; a slope of slow arrivals propelling
Downward toward the distant terminal
Became the single constellation visible.

The Upper Room

It's been so quiet up there for so long
I sometimes wonder if the tenants left.
But lying in my bed, propped on the soft
Pillow of sleep, I'll hear a faucet go on,
Or something like a chair scraping the floor,
Or the thin click of a door. After the noise,
I hold my breath to wait for a voice or sneeze,
A laugh, a muffled come-cry—something more

Definitively human. And so it is
That I myself have grown into the habit
Of silence, whispering into the phone,
Muting the TV, so as not to miss
The evidence. One night I thought I had it:
Strains of a song I'd known—then it was gone.

Vision (Sweet Recess)

It's odd: the sacred world can pass for years
Unseen, then fill your eyes, stopping you still,
As if God had stooped to whisper in your ears
Look there: the nuthatch on the kitchen sill,
Feathers ruffled to fatness against the cold;
The neighbor's listing shed, its siding (white
Once, gray and peeling now) recast in gold
By early evening's kind alchemic light;

Or one you love, framed in the entryway,
Wholly herself, and you for once abstracted
From fierce desire, its lenses and scaffoldings,
And left by language, which will not convey
The sense of stupid wonder that, though muted,
Fills the cage of your ribs with a riff of wings.

Weighing Light

Often the slightest gesture is most telling,
As when he reaches tenderly in passing
To pluck the yellow leaf from the dark fall

Of her hair, or even the absence of all gesture:
The way she doesn't need to turn to know
Who, in this gathering of friends, has touched her.

It was as if he dreamed some private garden.
Perhaps he woke from it, mid-reach, to find
His hand too near her hair in this crowded yard,

And maybe even now she's shuttering in
(She's even better than you or I at that)
A storm of worry and recrimination—

Did anyone notice? how could he do that here!—
By seamlessly continuing to tell you
About her trip to see her favorite Vermeer

This morning in the Delft show at the Met:
"So now they say she isn't weighing pearls
Or gold or anything—it's just the light

Gleaming off empty scales." So much is hard
To know for sure. If I confronted her,
She'd say it was just a leaf—who could afford

To disagree? Could we? Now she's explaining
How the girl faces a mirror we can't see into
And how behind her hangs a gloomy painting

Of the Last Judgment: "Over her head God
Floats in a cloud," she says, "like a thought balloon."
But you don't hear. You're watching me. I nod.

You Are Here

On the darkening map of this moment,
I'm the traveler at the frayed edge,
camped by the weak fire; you're the restless

pale shape sleeping at the center.
Between us lie the forests of your grief.
There is no legend, no scale,

but I will be where you are when you wake,
in a clearing, red leaves trembling
around us, and we will speak,

after seasons of silence, like birds again.
I run my hands over bodies of water,
borders and time zones, toward you.

Geoffrey Brock's poems have appeared in the *Hudson Review*, *Poetry*, *PN Review*, *New England Review*, and *32 Poems*, as well as in several anthologies. He has held a Wallace Stegner Fellowship, an NEA Fellowship, and a Guggenheim Fellowship. *Disaffections*, his translation of Cesare Pavese's poetry, was named one of the "Best Books of 2003" by the *Los Angeles Times* and received both the PEN Center U.S.A. Translation Award and the MLA's Lois Roth Translation Award. He has also translated books by Roberto Calasso and Umberto Eco. Mr. Brock earned an M.F.A. from the University of Florida and a Ph.D. from the University of Pennsylvania, and he is now on the faculty of the Programs in Creative Writing and Translation at the University of Arkansas. His website is www.geoffreybrock.com.

The New Criterion is recognized as one of the foremost contemporary venues for poetry with a regard for traditional meter and form. The magazine was thus an early leader in that poetic renaissance that has come to be called the New Formalism. Building upon its commitment to serious poetry, *The New Criterion* in 2000 established an annual prize, which carries an award of $3000. Geoffrey Brock is the fifth winner.